THE ULTIMATE
HOUSTON TEXANS
TRIVIA BOOK

A Collection of Amazing Trivia Quizzes
and Fun Facts for Die-Hard Texans Fans!

Ray Walker

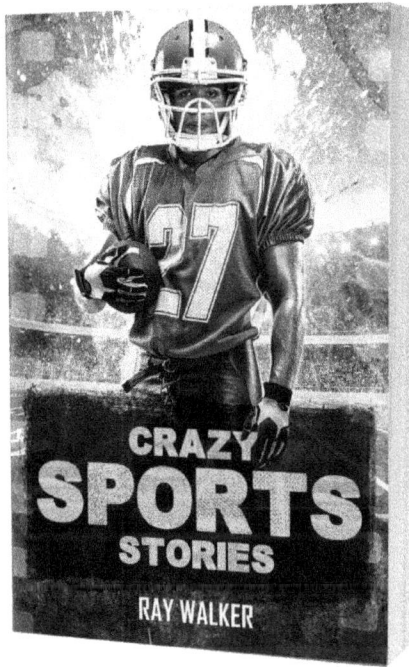

CONTENTS

INTRODUCTION

Obviously, you're forever inspired by your favorite team. In this case, the team in lights is the Houston Texans, the latest NFL franchise. It was founded in 2002 in Houston, Texas, and is surely one of the best teams in the current National Football League. Although fans of the archrival Tennessee Titans might want to argue over your claim just a bit.

Houston, nicknamed "Space City" because of its strong connection to NASA, has long been host to exciting sports and winning pro teams: the Houston Astros in Major League Baseball, the Houston Rockets in the National Basketball Association, and Dynamo F.C. in Major League Soccer, together with the Dash in the National Women's Soccer League. Multinational companies like ConocoPhillips, Halliburton, Hewlett Packard, Phillips 66, and Sysco make this major city even more dynamic.

But your Houston Texans are extra special. There's no place in the world to play and watch football like their unique home field, NRG Stadium (formerly Reliant), located near the Astrodome—especially when it's filled with 72,220 riotous Texans fans.

This year, the Texans will celebrate 19 years of existence at (or at least near!) the peak of the pro football world, and you'll be there, armed with all the trivia and fun facts about their colorful players, big signings and trades, and the incredible emotional highs and lows of a pro sports team. The Texans have already had their fair share, including the team's first postseason victory over the Bengals in 2012 and, a year before, clinching their first AFC South division championship in 2011. Hope springs eternal in the Lone Star State.

Clearly, you may use the book as you wish. Each chapter contains 20 quiz questions in a mix of multiple-choice and true-false formats, an answer key (Don't worry, it's on a separate page!), and a section of 10 "Did You Know?" facts about the team.

For the record, the information and stats in this book are current up to the beginning of 2021. The Houston Texans will surely break more records and win more awards as the seasons march on, so keep this in mind when you're watching the next game with your friends. You never quite know: someone could suddenly start a conversation with, "Did you know…?" And you'll be ready.

CHAPTER 1:

ORIGINS & HISTORY

QUIZ TIME!

1. The Houston Texans arrived in town in 2002 to replace the city's previous NFL franchise, the Houston Oilers. What team did the Oilers become?

   a. Arizona Cardinals

   b. Los Angeles Chargers

   c. Seattle Seahawks

   d. Tennessee Titans

2. Which other pro sports league bypassed the city of Houston in 1997, thus opening the way for a new NFL franchise?

   a. Major League Soccer

   b. National Basketball Association

   c. National Bowling Federation

   d. National Hockey League

3. Which Houston businessman was largely responsible for luring the NFL back to Houston in 2000?

a. Bud Adams

b. Bob McNair

c. Michael Ovitz

d. Paul Tagliabue

4. At that time, a number of team names were trademarked for possible use by the franchise, including the Apollos, Bobcats, Challengers, Colt 45's, Energy, Hurricanes, Roughnecks, Roughriders, Roustabouts, Stallions, Storm-cats, Texans, Texians, Toros, Wildcats, Wildcatters, and Wranglers.

a. True

b. False

5. The name "Texans" was finally chosen over the "Stallions" as horse imagery was considered already overused in the NFL. Which of the following teams do NOT use a name related to horses?

a. Denver Broncos

b. Green Bay Packers

c. Indianapolis Colts

d. San Diego Chargers

6. Who was named the Texans' first head coach in January 2001?

a. Dom Capers

b. Dick Jauron

c. Jim Mora

d. Dick Vermeil

7. In their first home game in 2002, which opponent did the Texans sneak by in a "shock" victory?

   a. Carolina Panthers
   b. Dallas Cowboys
   c. Jacksonville Jaguars
   d. New Orleans Saints

8. Back in 1998, which of the following cities and large media markets was Houston NOT competing with for an NFL franchise?

   a. Cleveland
   b. Los Angeles
   c. Nashville
   d. Toronto

9. How much was the winning bid from Houston NFL Holdings in 1999 that secured the NFL's 32nd franchise for the city?

   a. $450 million
   b. $540 million
   c. $700 million
   d. $888 million

10. The Texans also managed to beat the Steelers in Pittsburgh in their inaugural 2002 season, despite a record-setting low number of total yards. What was the measly total ground out by Houston runners?

   a. 40
   b. 46

c. 58

d. 64

11. Which team did Houston upset in its 2003 home opener, making it the first franchise ever to win its first two home openers?

    a. Miami Dolphins

    b. Minnesota Vikings

    c. New England Patriots

    d. San Francisco 49ers

12. Houston's first season was considered a success, despite David Carr being sacked an NFL record 85 times and the realization that Tony Boselli, the player they hoped would protect their young quarterback, would never play a single down of football for the team.

    a. True

    b. False

13. In what year did the Texans finally secure their first-ever winning streak of two games?

    a. 2003

    b. 2004

    c. 2005

    d. 2007

14. What was the name of the Houston executive who started to come under fire in 2005 for his "lackluster" draft picks?

    a. Charley Casserly

    b. Andre Johnson

c. Chris Palmer

d. Chuck Watson

15. Late in 2005, the Texans came into a game together with another team that had one of the two worst records in the NFL. The loser would "win" the right to choose USC running back Reggie Bush in the 2006 NFL Draft. Which of the following teams was the sorry opponent?

a. Cincinnati Bengals

b. Cleveland Browns

c. San Diego Chargers

d. San Francisco 49ers

16. One 2005 bright spot in Houston was the outstanding rookie season by kick returner Jerome Mathis, who returned two kicks for touchdowns. How many yards was his return against the Kansas City Chiefs?

a. 77

b. 88

c. 99

d. 102

17. In 2004, Tony Wyllie and the Texans' PR office were presented with the team's first special award, handed out by the Pro Football Writers of America. Who was the award named after?

a. Roone Arledge

b. King Fisher

c. Vince Lombardi

d. Pete Rozelle

18. In December 2015, Houston's 14th attempt to win in Indianapolis started badly. But a motivated third-string quarterback, Brandon Weeden, and a stifling defense turned the game around, leading to a surprising win over the rival Colts.

    a. True
    b. False

19. Which offensive coordinator, also a Houston native and Texas A&M alum, was hired to take the reins of the Texans in 2006?

    a. John Elway
    b. Gary Kubiak
    c. Bill O'Brien
    d. Wade Phillips

20. Rather than draft Reggie Bush in 2006, there was a mountain of support to pick local hero Vince Young after his team had knocked off Bush's USC in the Rose Bowl. Where did Young play his college football?

    a. Southern Methodist University
    b. Texas A&M
    c. Texas Christian University
    d. University of Texas

QUIZ ANSWERS

1. D – Tennessee Titans

2. D – National Hockey League

3. B – Bob McNair

4. A – True

5. B – Green Bay Packers

6. A – Dom Capers

7. B – Dallas Cowboys

8. C – Nashville

9. C – $700 million

10. B – 46

11. A – Miami Dolphins

12. B – False (Carr was "only" sacked a record 76 times.)

13. B – 2004

14. A – Charley Casserly

15. D – San Francisco 49ers

16. C – 99

17. D – Pete Rozelle

18. A – True

19. B – Gary Kubiak

20. D – University of Texas

DID YOU KNOW?

1. Despite some growing pains in their first decade of existence, the Texans became a dominant team in the NFL's AFC South Division in the 2010s, but have yet to appear in a Super Bowl.

2. In 1997, Houston was suddenly without professional football for the first time since 1959. Houston Oilers owner Bud Adams received final approval to move his team to Tennessee. The city of Houston, Harris County, and other parties filed a lawsuit that was settled after Adams paid millions of dollars for rudely skipping town.

3. Later in the same year, officials from Houston Livestock Show and Rodeo (HLS&R) declared that they would push for a domed stadium as part of the effort to bring the NFL back to Houston.

4. On October 6, 1999, businessman Bob McNair's persistence finally hit pay dirt: NFL owners voted 29-0 to accept his offer over various bids from Los Angeles. In addition, Houston would get to host the 2004 Super Bowl.

5. On March 9, 2000, Houston feted the official ground-breaking of Reliant Stadium. The 69,500-seat state-of-the-art facility became the NFL's first stadium with a retractable roof.

6. The team name, the Houston Texans, was selected as "something unique to Houston and the NFL," as well as representing the bravery of Texas natives.

7. Prior to 2001, new Houston head man Dom Capers served for two seasons as the Jacksonville Jaguars' defensive coordinator. From 1995 to 1998, Capers toiled as the head coach of the then-expansion Carolina Panthers.

8. The Texans stunned the NFL world just before the 2006 NFL Draft by announcing that North Carolina State defensive end Mario Williams—not runner Reggie Bush or quarterback Vince Young—would be the team's first draft choice.

9. By drafting Mario Williams in 2006, the Texans took care of their greatest need. But it would turn out to be a PR nightmare that haunted them for much of the following season.

10. In February 2006, after receiving Gary Kubiak's vote of confidence, the Texans paid an $8 million bonus option to David Carr, guaranteeing he would remain a Texan.

CHAPTER 2:

THE NUMBERS GAME

QUIZ TIME!

1. J.J. Watt wore number 99 during his entire Houston career. Three times NFL Defensive Player of the Year, five times a First Team All-Pro, and the Walter Payton Man of the Year in 2017, Watt attended what university?

   a. Utah
   b. Washington
   c. Wisconsin
   d. Wyoming

2. Wide receiver Andre Johnson sported number 80. When he played 16 games in a season, which he did on seven occasions, how many times did he exceed 1,000 yards receiving?

   a. 4
   b. 5
   c. 6
   d. 7

3. Deshaun Watson dazzled in 2018: starting all 16 games, he guided Houston to 11 wins and an AFC South title while completing 68.3% of his throws for 4,165 yards, with 26 touchdown passes to only nine interceptions. On top of that, he ran for five scores and earned the first Pro Bowl nod of his career.

   a. True
   b. False

4. The Texan mascot wears number 1, but has never actually played in a game. On the other hand, he's done numerous high-wire stunts, energized the crowd, dressed up in a bunch of costumes, and performed good deeds off the field. What's his name?

   a. Harry
   b. Henry
   c. Tex
   d. Toro

5. After helping Denver to a Super Bowl win in 2016, Brock Osweiler signed with Houston for a cool $72 million. However, he went on to launch a franchise-record number of picks his first season. How many?

   a. 12
   b. 16
   c. 20
   d. 23

6. B.J. Daniels, wearing jersey number 2, was part of a 2015 "quarterback carousel" in Houston. How many quarter-backs took snaps as the Texans won the AFC South?

   a. 9
   b. 7
   c. 6
   d. 5

7. With number 6 on his back, T.J. Yates also called some signals in 2015. Which team (then sporting an 8-0 record) did Yates help knock from the undefeated ranks that year?

   a. Atlanta Falcons
   b. Chicago Bears
   c. Cincinnati Bengals
   d. Detroit Lions

8. This undrafted player led the NFL in scoring with 150 points in Houston's 2018 AFC South championship season, connecting on 37 of 42 field goal tries and making all but two of his 41 point-after tries. Finally, he split the uprights on all 21 of his attempts inside 40 yards. Who was he?

   a. Ka'imi Fairbairn
   b. Donnie Jones
   c. Neil Rackers
   d. Matt Turk

9. Justin Reid was the first Texan drafted in 2018. As a rookie, Reid had 81 tackles, picked off three passes, and broke up 10 more. How many yards was his interception runback against Washington for a touchdown that year?

    a. 104
    b. 101
    c. 97
    d. 94

10. To date, long snapper Jon Weeks has played in 160 games as a Texan. Who's the only player to have figured in more games for Houston, with 169?

    a. Brian Cushing
    b. Kareem Jackson
    c. Andre Johnson
    d. DeMeco Ryans

11. In 2016, which Texan was the only player in the NFL to finish with 100 or more tackles and five or more sacks?

    a. Danny Clark
    b. Drew Hodgdon
    c. Bernardrick McKinney
    d. Chris Myers

12. Linebacker Kenneth Pettway was Houston's 7th draft pick in 2005. He made the roster but never saw game action. How many players constitute the "normal" roster?

    a. 58
    b. 53

c. 48

d. 40

13. Which Houston player won a Super Bowl ring as a starter with the Ravens in 2000 and, during his final NFL season in 2005, helped the Seahawks make it to their first-ever Super Bowl? He retired after nine NFL seasons and then spent the 2013 preseason with the Texans as a scouting intern.

   a. Mike Brisiel

   b. Greg Mancz

   c. Chester Pitts

   d. Jamie Sharper

14. Offensive lineman Ryan Schau featured in the Texans' first road win ever on October 27, 2002—a 21-19 nail-biter. Who was the opponent?

   a. Arizona Cardinals

   b. Jacksonville Jaguars

   c. Oakland Raiders

   d. San Francisco 49ers

15. In the spring of 2006, Kevin Walter came to Houston as a free agent. Over the next seven seasons, he caught 24 touchdowns and 326 passes for 4,083 yards. He snagged a last-second pass from T.J. Yates to beat Cincinnati in December 2011, and clinch the AFC South.

   a. True

   b. False

16. Besides on-field accomplishments, one prominent Houston player founded a charitable foundation and made annual trips to Toys "R" Us, where he "enabled 12 underserved youth from Harris County's Department of Family Protective Services to pick out holiday gifts." Who was this hero?

    a. Andre Johnson
    b. David Johnson
    c. Matt Schaub
    d. J.J. Watt

17. Arian Isa Foster is the Texans' all-time rushing leader with 6,527 yards on 1,476 attempts. Where was Foster born?

    a. Denver, Colorado
    b. Fort Collins, Colorado
    c. Albuquerque, New Mexico
    d. Santa Fe, New Mexico

18. On Christmas Eve 2006, Kris Brown nailed a lengthy field goal as time expired to give the Texans their first-ever win over their rivals from Indianapolis. How long was the winning boot?

    a. 45 yards
    b. 48 yards
    c. 51 yards
    d. 55 yards

19. In each of the first two games of the 2007 season, Matt Schaub threw for over 220 yards, achieved a 71% completion percentage, and received a quarterback rating of over 100, while Houston went to 2-0 for the first time in franchise history. Who was Houston's first "victim" in 2007?

    a. Atlanta Falcons
    b. Carolina Panthers
    c. Kansas City Chiefs
    d. Pittsburgh Steelers

20. Besides Andre Johnson and J.J. Watt, DeAndre Hopkins has the third-highest Approximate Value (AV) in the history of the Texans.

    a. True
    b. False

QUIZ ANSWERS

1. C – Wisconsin
2. C – 6
3. A – True
4. D – Toro
5. B – 16
6. B – 7
7. C – Cincinnati Bengals
8. A – Ka'imi Fairbairn
9. B – 101
10. C – Andre Johnson
11. C – Bernardrick McKinney
12. B – 53
13. D – Jamie Sharper
14. B – Jacksonville Jaguars
15. A – True
16. A – Andre Johnson
17. C – Albuquerque, New Mexico
18. B – 48 yards
19. C – Kansas City Chiefs
20. B – False (Duane Brown has the third-highest AV in Houston's brief history.)

DID YOU KNOW?

1. In the 2019 postseason, DeAndre Hopkins ran wild in the Wild Card round against the Buffalo Bills, recording six receptions for 90 yards and a two-point conversion in the 22-19 overtime victory.

2. Shane Lechler grew up in nearby East Bernard, played at Texas A&M, and averaged 47.6 yards per punt as a Texan. Considered one of the best punters in NFL history, he was a six-time All-Pro punter as a Raider and earned seven Pro Bowl nods.

3. In the final game of a disastrous 2013 season for Houston, Ray Graham carried the ball four times for eight yards and caught a pass for 12 yards in a Texans defeat at Tennessee. It turned out to be the only action of Graham's NFL career.

4. When Hurricane Harvey hit in 2017, J.J. Watt fronted a campaign that brought in more than $40 million for emergency relief, and his efforts earned him the Walter Payton Man of the Year award. During the Covid pandemic, Watt and his wife Kealia turned over $350,000 to the Houston Food Bank.
   (https://www.houstontexans.com/news/99-history-of-texans-numbers)

5. An original Texan, Jamie Sharper came to the team in the 2002 Expansion Draft from Baltimore. With Houston, his

best season came in 2003, when he led the NFL with 164 tackles. Sharper was named the club's MVP and also became the Texans' Walter Payton Man of the Year nominee.

6. Chester Pitts still holds the franchise mark for consecutive starts, with 114. In addition, he started every game from the inaugural win over the Cowboys through Week 2 of 2009, when he hurt his knee. Pitts appears on the pregame and halftime shows during NRG Stadium home games and is a frequent guest on *Texans Extra Points*.

7. Picked in the 3rd round of the 2006 NFL Draft, right tackle Eric Winston was one of the finest linemen in team history. He started the last seven games as a rookie and then every game after that in his time as a Texan. He played high school ball for Texas state champs, the Midland Lee Rebels.

8. On the day the Astros won Game 7 of the World Series in 2017, defensive lineman Angelo Blackson inked a free-agent deal with the Texans. Blackson started 20 times for Houston, with 15 of those games coming in the 2019 AFC South championship year.

9. In 2019, the Texans went 9-3 in one-score games, including the big postseason win against Buffalo. They won 2.2 more games than expected based on their point differential. Their performance was mediocre. The offense was average, the defense terrible, and the special teams great.

10. The 2020 season was a different ballgame: Houston finished at 4-12 and tied for 28th in turnover differential at -9. The defense forced only nine turnovers, and the porous secondary intercepted only two passes.

CHAPTER 3:

CALLING THE SIGNALS

QUIZ TIME!

1. Matt Schaub started 2007 well but was eventually sidelined with injuries. Who stepped up to help lead the Texans to their first .500 record in history?

    a. David Carr
    b. Matt Leinart
    c. Ryan Mallett
    d. Sage Rosenfels

2. Which Houston quarterback recorded the most starts (88) in franchise history?

    a. Ryan Fitzpatrick
    b. Case Keenum
    c. Matt Schaub
    d. Deshaun Watson

3. In the humble history of the Houston Texans, one quarterback started a single game and came out a loser. Who was he?

a. Tony Banks

b. A.J. McCarron

c. Dave Ragone

d. Brandon Weeden

4. Deshaun Watson is one of only four NFL quarterbacks with a career passing rating of over 100. Which of the following quarterbacks does NOT have a rating over 100?

a. Bart Starr

b. Patrick Mahomes

c. Aaron Rodgers

d. Russell Wilson

5. Houston's Tyrod Taylor was previously a backup with Baltimore, including during the Ravens' 2013 Super Bowl victory over the 49ers. Which Baltimore starter did he support?

a. Joe Flacco

b. Lamar Jackson

c. Steve McNair

d. Troy Smith

6. Tony Banks was signed by Houston to back up David Carr at quarterback, which he did for four years. Which of the following teams did he NOT previously suit up for?

a. Buffalo Bills

b. Dallas Cowboys

c. New England Patriots

d. Washington Redskins

7. As well as being a member of the National Honor Society, Sage Rosenfels excelled in a number of sports in his Iowa high school, Maquoketa. Which of the following did he NOT play?

    a. Basketball
    b. Football
    c. Tennis
    d. Wrestling

8. Matt Leinart played quarterback for Houston in 2010 and 2011. What was the name of the Barstool Sports podcast he often appeared in from 2014 onwards?

    a. I Fell Off My Barstool Too
    b. Pardon My French
    c. Pardon My Take
    d. Please Pass the Mustard

9. After serving as the assistant quarterbacks coach for Houston in 2020, former quarterback T.J. Yates moved to the Atlanta Falcons franchise, where he became the passing game specialist.

    a. True
    b. False

10. While Case Keenum aired it out in college at Houston, in which of the following categories did he NOT become the all-time NCAA leader?

    a. Completions
    b. Passing yards

c. Total offense

d. Touchdowns

11. With Texans starter Matt Schaub knocked out of action in 2013, Keenum stepped into the fray and tossed his first touchdown as a pro. Who was the receiver of the 29-yard strike?

    a. DeAndre Hopkins

    b. Lester Jean

    c. Keyshawn Martin

    d. DeVier Posey

12. Ryan Fitzpatrick played college football for the Princeton Tigers from 2001 to 2004 and was the school's first quarterback to rush for over 1,000 career yards.

    a. True

    b. False

13. After he played college football with the Arkansas Razorbacks, which team drafted Ryan Mallett before he eventually made it into the Texans' lineup?

    a. Baltimore Ravens

    b. Indianapolis Colts

    c. New England Patriots

    d. Seattle Seahawks

14. When Mallett was named the starting quarterback for Houston in 2014, effectively replacing Ryan Fitzpatrick, who was the coach who gave him the nod?

    a. Dom Capers

    b. Gary Kubiak

   c. Bill O'Brien

   d. Wade Phillips

15. Brian Hoyer took snaps for Houston in 2015. What is his actual first name?

   a. Allen

   b. Arthur

   c. Axel

   d. Axle

16. Before settling in as an NFL quarterback, Brandon Weeden gave pro baseball a shot. But due to injuries and poor performance, he gave up on hardball in 2006. Which was his last team in the California League?

   a. High Desert Mavericks

   b. Lancaster JetHawks

   c. Modesto Nuts

   d. Stockton Ports

17. Late in 2016, an ineffective Brock Osweiler was benched in favor of Tom Savage, who then commanded the Texans in a thrilling 21-20 come-from-behind win. Who was the opponent?

   a. Atlanta Falcons

   b. Dallas Cowboys

   c. Jacksonville Jaguars

   d. Washington Football Team

18. When A.J. McCarron was only five years old, he was seriously injured in a jet ski accident and almost lost his life. Where was A.J. born?

a. Gulf Shores, Alabama

b. Mobile, Alabama

c. Montgomery, Alabama

d. Tuscaloosa, Alabama

19. McCarron appeared in a single play for Houston when he briefly replaced Deshaun Watson in 2020. What happened during the play?

a. He fumbled the ball for a loss.

b. He faked a pass and bootlegged for 45 yards.

c. He threw a touchdown pass.

d. He was sacked for a turnover on downs.

20. Deshaun Watson finished first in the NFL in passing yards in the 2020 season. He became the first player to lead the league in passing yards on a team with at least 12 losses since _____ of the Oakland Raiders in 1997. Whose name is missing?

a. Jeff George

b. Todd Marinovich

c. Jim Plunkett

d. Kenny Stabler

QUIZ ANSWERS

1. D – Sage Rosenfels

2. C – Matt Schaub

3. B – A.J. McCarron

4. A – Bart Starr

5. A – Joe Flacco

6. C – New England Patriots

7. D – Wrestling

8. C – *Pardon My Take*

9. A – True

10. C – Total offense

11. A – DeAndre Hopkins

12. B – False (Fitzpatrick was the first quarterback to rush for 1,000 yards for the Harvard Crimson.)

13. C – New England Patriots

14. C – Bill O'Brien

15. C – Axel

16. A – High Desert Mavericks

17. C – Jacksonville Jaguars

18. B – Mobile, Alabama

19. D – He was sacked for a turnover on downs.

20. A – Jeff George

DID YOU KNOW?

1. During his senior year at Fresno State in 2001, Derek Carr won the Johnny Unitas Golden Arm Award and was a finalist for the Heisman Trophy, finishing fifth.

2. Carr was sacked 76 times in his rookie season in 2002, an NFL record for the most times a quarterback had been sacked in a season. He also established the NFL record for fumble recoveries in a single season, recovering 12 of his own. Both records still stood as of 2021.

3. In 2018, Deshaun Watson led the league in average time spent in the pocket and was second in average time before launching the ball. This was a major factor contributing to his facing the most dropbacks under pressure (281) and tying for fifth-most sacks in a single season in NFL history, with 62.

4. In the 2019 Wild Card round against the Buffalo Bills, Watson commandeered the Texans back from a 16-0 deficit to win 22-19 in overtime, despite seven sacks.

5. T.J. Yates holds several University of North Carolina records, including those for total career passing yards and single-season passing yards, having broken the marks set by his predecessor Darian Durant during his stint as a Tar Heel.

6. After signing with the Texans as an undrafted free agent in 2012, Case Keenum threw for 1,760 yards and nine touchdowns in the eight games he started for Houston, before being waived before the 2014 season.

7. Regarded as a journeyman quarterback, Ryan Fitzpatrick started and threw touchdown passes for eight different teams during his 16-season career, the most of any NFL quarterback.

8. Despite playing with such a variety of teams, Fitzpatrick never made it to the playoffs. His wildly different performances in games led him to be referred to alternately as "Fitzmagic" and "Fitztragic."

9. On January 3, 2016, Brian Hoyer led Houston to its first playoff berth and AFC South title since 2012 with a resounding 30-6 victory over the Jaguars. Then, when the Texans played in the first AFC Wild Card game against the Chiefs, Hoyer struggled, throwing for only 136 yards with four interceptions. Houston was shut out by Kansas City, 30-0.

10. On November 30, 2014, against the Tennessee Titans, rookie Tom Savage appeared in a game for the first time and participated in two exciting "kneel-down" plays.

CHAPTER 4:

BETWEEN THE TACKLES

QUIZ TIME!

1. In the 2010 season opener against the Colts, Arian Foster blasted out of the blocks, sprinting for the most yards in a single game of any Texans runner ever. How many did he gain?

    a. 180

    b. 196

    c. 231

    d. 247

2. Unfortunately, Foster tore something against the Dolphins in 2014, which effectively ended his stint with Houston. Ironically, Miami opted to pick him up in 2016. What body part did he tear?

    a. Achilles tendon

    b. Anterior cruciate ligament

    c. Elbow tendon

    d. Rib muscles

3. Domanick Williams tore up the turf running for Houston until he injured his knee just before his third straight 1,000-yard season. What was his name during his playing days?

    a. Domanick Davies
    b. Domanick Davis
    c. Dominique Wilkins
    d. Donald Williams

4. Domanick didn't win the official NFL Rookie of the Year award in 2003. However, he was given a secondary Rookie of the Year award in a vote by fans. Which company sponsored this vote?

    a. Ben & Jerry's
    b. Bud Light
    c. Diet Pepsi
    d. Mountain Dew

5. When the Texans released Foster after the 2015 season, they wasted no time signing another rapid ground-gainer to a $26 million deal. Who was the man that gained 106 yards on a career-high 28 carries in his debut?

    a. Ron Dayne
    b. David Johnson
    c. Lamar Miller
    d. Ben Tate

6. In his first game as a Texan, against Washington in 2014, runner Alfred Blue saw special teams duty, blocked a

punt, and returned it for a touchdown. Who was the hapless punter?

a. Dan Carpenter
b. Nick Folk
c. Stephen Gostkowski
d. Tress Way

7. In 2008, Steve Slaton didn't start the first game of his career, but his role changed dramatically after he outgained veteran Ahman Green in the opening game against the Steelers. What followed were 15 straight starts of brilliance.

a. True
b. False

8. Drafted by the Eagles, Ryan Moats also ran for the Cardinals, Texans, and Vikings. What other sport did he turn to after retiring from the gridiron?

a. Badminton
b. Greco-Roman wrestling
c. Rugby
d. Track and field

9. Against the Jacksonville Jaguars in November 2006, Samkon Gado picked up a critical fourth-down conversion in the fourth quarter to secure a 13-10 win for the Texans. What does his first name mean in his native Tangale (Nigerian) language?

a. Honesty
b. Honor

c. Justice

d. Truth

10. While playing collegiate football for the Notre Dame Fighting Irish, Darius Walker set the record for most receptions in a single season (2006) by a running back. How many passes did he snag?

a. 34

b. 45

c. 56

d. 68

11. Derrick Ward earned a Super Bowl ring playing for the Giants (unfortunately, not the Texans) after the 2007 season. Which opponent did New York squeak by in that game?

a. Dallas Cowboys

b. New England Patriots

c. Philadelphia Eagles

d. San Francisco 49ers

12. When Phillip Lindsay agreed to a one-year contract in March 2021 to bolster the Texans' ground game, how much did the former Denver running back rake in?

a. $1.5 million

b. $2.25 million

c. $3.25 million

d. $4.75 million

13. When describing Mark Ingram's running style versus that of the fleet-footed Lindsay, the former is seen as more "the _____, hammer-the-center-of-the-line-style back." What's missing?

    a. Jackrabbit
    b. Pile driver
    c. Steamroller
    d. Workhorse

14. In March 2020, the Texans acquired runner David Johnson from the Cardinals in exchange for DeAndre Hopkins and some draft picks. At which university did Johnson excel?

    a. North Dakota
    b. Northern Illinois
    c. Northern Iowa
    d. Northern New Mexico

15. Carlos Hyde ran rampant for 160 yards against the Jaguars in a Week 9 win in 2019, including a 58-yard romp after which Hyde lost the ball for a touchback. Where was that game played?

    a. NRG Stadium, Houston
    b. TDECU Stadium, Houston
    c. TIAA Bank Field, Jacksonville
    d. Wembley Stadium, London

16. Houston runner Duke Johnson ran for some impressive yardage in his career as a Miami Hurricane from 2012 to 2014. Whose school rushing record for all-time yards did he finally break?

a. Ottis Anderson

b. Frank Gore

c. Edgerrin James

d. Clinton Portis

17. On his final collegiate play, Cullen Gillaspia scored a 13-yard rushing touchdown in Texas A&M's 52-13 win over North Carolina State in the Gator Bowl, the first touchdown by a 12th man in the program's history.

a. True

b. False

18. When D'Onta Foreman starred at Texas City High School in 2013, he was ranked the 67th best running back nationally. On the other hand, what was his ranking that same year as the best player in the state of Texas by 247Sports?

a. 10th

b. 30th

c. 68th

d. 125th

19. Texans runner Tyler Ervin celebrated his final college game with the San Jose State Spartans by returning a punt 85 yards in a win over Georgia State. What was the name of that 2015 bowl game?

a. Cure Bowl

b. Gatorade Bowl

c. Punch Bowl

d. Tangerine Bowl

20. Kenny Dilliard didn't quite make the grade as a Houston runner in 2016. He fizzled with Washington as well. What was the final pro team he tried to catch on with?

   a. Arizona Hotshots
   b. Atlanta Legends
   c. Memphis Express
   d. Salt Lake Stallions

QUIZ ANSWERS

1. C – 231

2. A – Achilles tendon

3. B – Domanick Davis

4. C – Diet Pepsi

5. C – Lamar Miller

6. D – Tress Way

7. A – True

8. C – Rugby

9. D – Truth

10. C – 56

11. B – New England Patriots

12. C – $3.25 million

13. D – Workhorse

14. C – Northern Iowa

15. D – Wembley Stadium, London

16. A – Ottis Anderson

17. A – True

18. D – 125th

19. A – Cure Bowl

20. C – Memphis Express

DID YOU KNOW?

1. Arian Foster had three consecutive 1,000-yard seasons, from 2010 to 2012, and he scored at least 10 rushing touchdowns in each of those seasons. In 2010, he led the NFL with 1,616 rushing yards and 16 touchdowns, in addition to 393 touches and 2,220 total offensive yards.

2. In his Houston career, Foster carried the ball 1,454 times for 6,472 yards and 54 touchdowns, all of which stand as franchise records. He added another 2,268 yards and 14 touchdowns on 249 receptions for a total of 8,740 offensive yards.

3. Due to his versatility, Domanick Williams had 24 games with at least 100 yards of total offense, even though he only broke the 100-yard rushing barrier 11 times.

4. Lamar Miller's greatest Houston highlight came in the 2018 season: He rambled 97 yards for a touchdown against the Titans, which was the longest play in franchise history. It was the second 97-yard touchdown of his career; the first came in a 2014 game against the Jets during his time with Miami, leaving him as the only player in NFL history with two touchdowns of more than 95 yards.

5. Alfred Blue's exceptional game as a 2014 rookie also immortalized his name in the franchise record book. His 36 attempts is the most recorded by a Texans running

back, and his 156 yards tied the single-game record for rookies.

6. Stave Slaton entered 2009 as a starter, but he lost six fumbles in almost as many games. It was later discovered that a nerve issue in his neck was the reason he lost his grip on the football and fumbled so often.

7. In Week 8 of the 2009 season, Ryan Moats scored three touchdowns after replacing starting running back Steve Slaton. Moats ended up with 126 yards on 23 carries.

8. In 2007, Ahman Green was reunited with his former head coach and former Texans assistant head coach Mike Sherman, along with former Packers running back, Samkon Gado. Green was asked to handle most of the load at running back after the 2006 season when the Texans used a "running back by committee" approach.

9. Ben Tate dashed for 115 yards against the Cleveland Browns in Week 9 of the 2009 season, while Arian Foster ran for 124 yards in the same game. Together, they led the Texans to 261 yards on the ground, a franchise record.

10. Known as the "Great Dayne" and the "Dayne Train" throughout his college years, Ron Dayne was the starting running back all four years at Wisconsin, and he won the Heisman Trophy in his final year (1999).

CHAPTER 5:

CATCHING THE BALL

QUIZ TIME!

1. Andre Johnson's breakout season in Houston came when he combined with quarterback David Carr for 1,142 yards on 79 catches, with six touchdowns, and he made his first Pro Bowl. What year was it?

   a. 2000

   b. 2002

   c. 2004

   d. 2008

2. In 2009, Johnson once again led the league in receiving yards with 1,569 on 101 receptions and a career-high nine touchdowns. Which other star did he join as the only two receivers since the merger to lead the league in receiving yards in two straight seasons?

   a. Cris Carter

   b. Larry Fitzgerald Jr.

   c. Calvin Johnson

   d. Jerry Rice

3. DeAndre Hopkins entered "the best wide receiver in the NFL" debate once and for all with a ridiculous 2018 season, including 115 catches. How many drops did he have that sparkling season?

    a. 9
    b. 6
    c. 4
    d. 0

4. Why did DeAndre's mother bestow the unusual nickname "Nuk" on the young receiver?

    a. Due to his favorite pacifier brand as a baby
    b. Due to his favorite popsicle as a kid
    c. Due to his large forehead
    d. Due to his love of movies about nuclear warfare as a teen

5. Despite all his injuries, this 1st round Notre Dame product still snagged 156 passes for 2,231 yards (a 13.7-yard average), 16 touchdowns, and 300 punt return yards (including a game where he scored on a pass play and a punt return, becoming the only Texan in history to do so). Who's the player in question?

    a. Amari Cooper
    b. Will Fuller V
    c. Tommy Reese
    d. Nate Washington

6. In addition to Houston, Corey Bradford played for Green Bay, Detroit, and Washington. How many receiving touchdowns did he haul in during his career?

   a. 14
   b. 19
   c. 25
   d. 37

7. Randall Ladonald Cobb II has been on the receiving end of Houston passes since 2020. Which extra jobs below did he NOT help his father, Randall Cobb Sr., with while growing near Marysville, Tennessee?

   a. Fixing pickup trucks
   b. Installing ceramic tile floors
   c. Mowing lawns
   d. Plowing snow

8. On August 31, 2019, Kenny Still was traded by the Dolphins to the Texans. He then made his debut against another former team and hauled in a touchdown in a narrow 30-28 road loss. What was the team?

   a. Buffalo Bills
   b. Chicago Bears
   c. New Orleans Saints
   d. New York Giants

9. Signed by the Texans in 2016 as an undrafted free agent, Wendall Williams made the news when he blasted the 40-yard dash record. What was his unofficial time?

a. 3.97 seconds

b. 4.19 seconds

c. 4.33 seconds

d. 4.56 seconds

10. Keke Coutee made his NFL debut with Houston in Week 4 of 2018 against the Indianapolis Colts. He finished the game with 13 receptions for 109 yards. Coutee's 13 receptions was the most catches in any player's first game since the AFL-NFL merger in 1966.

a. True

b. False

11. Isaiah Coulter joined the Texans' receiving corps in 2020. What university did he attend?

a. Kentucky

b. Rhode Island

c. Rice

d. Vermont

12. Andre Roberts was an outstanding football and track athlete both at Spring Valley High School and The Citadel in South Carolina. He also played for six other pro franchises before joining Houston. Where was he born?

a. Columbia, South Carolina

b. Fairbanks, Alaska

c. Juneau, Alaska

d. Spartanburg, South Carolina

13. Which of the following teams did Donte Moncrief NOT play for before becoming a Houston Texan in 2021?

    a. Carolina Panthers
    b. Green Bay Packers
    c. Jacksonville Jaguars
    d. New England Patriots

14. Alex Michael Erickson had a record-breaking collegiate career at Wisconsin before being drafted by the Bengals in 2016. What was his college major?

    a. Agricultural business management
    b. Computer science
    c. Natural resources conservation
    d. Visual arts

15. Wide receiver Chris Moore had four reasonable seasons with the Baltimore Ravens before officially becoming a Texan. What was the potential value of the Houston contract he signed in 2021?

    a. $2.8 million
    b. $4.5 million
    c. $6 million
    d. $8 million

16. Tight end Jordan Akins had a dream to play major league baseball, especially after being drafted by the Texas Rangers. However, his anemic batting average in four minor-league seasons got him back to the gridiron. What was his BA?

a. .165

b. .187

c. .218

d. .232

17. In Week 10 of the 2020 season against the Cleveland Browns, Pharaoh Brown grabbed his first professional touchdown pass from Deshaun Watson. Alas, Houston still came out on the short end of the score. What was the final?

    a. 10-7

    b. 14-7

    c. 14-10

    d. 21-20

18. Receiver Chris Conley's father had a career in the US Air Force, and Chris was born in Adana, Turkey. He was raised as a devout Christian and was named Christian at birth.

    a. True

    b. False

19. When Ryan Izzo played tight end at Pope John XXIII Regional High School in New Jersey, he drew little attention from D1 schools at first, and then Virginia Tech showed interest. How many other schools quickly followed suit?

    a. 10

    b. 15

    c. 20

    d. 30

20. Before playing tight end for the Texans and a variety of other NFL teams, Darren Fells only played basketball in college and professionally. Which NFL franchise was the first to sign him?

    a. Los Angeles Raiders
    b. San Diego Chargers
    c. San Francisco 49ers
    d. Seattle Seahawks

QUIZ ANSWERS

1. C – 2004

2. D – Jerry Rice

3. D – 0

4. A – Due to his favorite pacifier brand as a baby

5. B – Will Fuller V

6. C – 25

7. A – Fixing pickup trucks

8. C – New Orleans Saints

9. B – 4.19 seconds

10. A – False (Keke finished his debut with 11 catches, which set the record.)

11. B – Rhode Island

12. B – Fairbanks, Alaska

13. B – Green Bay Packers

14. A – Agricultural business management

15. D – $8 million

16. C – .218

17. A – 10-7

18. A – True

19. C – 20

20. D – Seattle Seahawks

DID YOU KNOW?

1. Houston receiver Andre Johnson was described this way: "The one, the only, the man, the myth, the legend, and all the other accolades heaped on top." Johnson was a beast on the field, while his heart for the Houston community could be rivaled only by J.J. Watt. Watching Johnson take needy kids on a Toys "R" Us shopping spree every year was always a holiday season highlight.

2. During his twelve years in Houston, the aforementioned Johnson caught 1,012 passes for 13,597 yards and 77 touchdowns, while delivering one serious smackdown of Titans defender Cortland Finnegan.

3. After Pro Bowler Andre Johnson was sidelined due to injury, Kevin Walter became Houston's number one pass catcher. In eight 2007 games, Walter had 40 catches for 512 yards and posted a career-high game at Jacksonville in Week 6 with 12 catches for 160 yards.

4. During his four-year stint in Houston, Corey Bradford caught 130 passes for 1,992 yards for a 15.3 yard per catch average, with 18 touchdowns and zero fumbles.

5. Brandin Cooks joined Brandon Marshall (drafted by Denver) as the only players in the history of the NFL to record 1,000-yard receiving seasons with four separate teams.

6. On September 8, 2011, in Green Bay's season-opening game against New Orleans, Randall Cobb became the first person born in the 1990s to play in the league. He recorded his first NFL touchdown on a 32-yard catch in the first quarter and followed it with a 108-yard kickoff runback in the third quarter that tied the record set for the NFL's longest-ever kickoff return by Ellis Hobbs of New England in 2007.

7. Wendall Williams dropped out of Hudson Valley Community College but was encouraged to enroll in 2011 at Herkimer County Community College, where he played basketball and track for the Generals. While at Herkimer, he was captain of the hoops squad, shooting 71% from the field, while pursuing an associate degree in business sports management.

8. Just in case you can't easily pronounce Houston receiver Key'vantanie Coutee's first name, his nickname is "Keke."

9. Chris Conley began playing football during his freshman year at North Paulding High School in Dallas, Georgia. He received numerous accolades there, including being an All-State chorus member. In elementary school, Conley won a regional third-grade science fair, received a $5,000 savings bond and a family trip to nationals in Chicago where he met TV repairman Bob Vila.

10. Tight end Michael Wodehouse "Kahale" Warring played college football at San Diego State and was drafted by the Texans in the 3rd round of the 2019 NFL Draft. Lucky for

the fans, he doesn't usually go by his full first name: "Kahalekuiokalani."

CHAPTER 6:

TRENCH WARFARE

QUIZ TIME!

1. J.J. Watt showed his versatility in and out of the trenches by playing defensive end and tackle, while also taking some snaps on the offensive side of the ball. In what year was he named *Sports Illustrated*'s Sportsperson of the Year?

   a. 2010
   b. 2013
   c. 2017
   d. 2020

2. J.J. Watt previously won the 2010 Lott IMPACT Trophy, presented every year to the college football defensive IMPACT player of the year, as a Wisconsin Badger. Which of the following words is NOT included in that acronym?

   a. Awareness
   b. Community

c. Integrity

d. Tenacity

3. When Jadeveon Clowney was only 13 years old with the South Pointe (SC) Stallions, he was already causing problems for his own offense in practice. His coach, Bobby Carroll, quipped that he was _____. What's missing?

a. Blasting blockers

b. Creating chaos

c. Making waves

d. Wreaking havoc

4. Antonio DeShonta Smith played defensive end for the Broncos, Cards, and Raiders, as well as the Texans. What was his nickname?

a. Battleship DeShonta

b. DeShonta Destroyer

c. Ninja Assassin

d. Smith the Smotherer

5. When Mario Williams was getting untracked in 2006, he recorded a monster game in Houston's 27-7 upset win over the Jags with a fumble recovery and a sack. Who was the Jacksonville quarterback he put under wraps?

a. Mark Brunell

b. Daunte Culpepper

c. David Garrard

d. Bryon Leftwich

6. Travis Johnson was projected by *Sports Illustrated* as a mid-first-round draft pick, while also being considered the best defensive tackle available. What was the year in question?

   a. 2002
   b. 2005
   c. 2007
   d. 2010

7. Amobi Okoye, a Nigerian-born defensive tackle, was selected by the Texans in the 2007 NFL Draft. He was the youngest player ever to be picked in the 1st round. How old was he at the time?

   a. 17
   b. 18
   c. 19
   d. 20

8. Nose tackle Shaun Cody participated in a Spike TV series titled *Super Agent,* in which a variety of sports agents competed for the right to work for him and negotiate his NFL contract.

   a. True
   b. False

9. When Terrell McClain played defensive end for the Texans in 2012, he finished with one fumble recovery and a career-high number of tackles. How many did he record in 16 games?

a. 16

b. 18

c. 21

d. 26

10. Brooks Reed replaced injured linebacker Mario Williams in the sixth game of his rookie year (2011), and he notched six tackles in his first start. Where was he born?

a. Flagstaff, Arizona

b. Taos, New Mexico

c. Tombstone, Arizona

d. Tucson, Arizona

11. Drafted by Houston in 2004, Jason Babin went on to play for numerous other NFL franchises, including two separate stints with one other team. How many teams did he play for in his career?

a. 10

b. 8

c. 6

d. 5

12. The following quote exalts Duane Brown's talent: "While Chris Myers was undoubtedly the best center in the Texans' history, Duane Brown is one of the best _____ players the team has ever seen." What's missing?

a. All-around

b. Defensive

c. Football

d. Offensive

13. In his seven seasons with the Texans, Chris Myers committed fewer penalties than another player in 2019 alone. In that span, Myers started 112 games, made two Pro Bowl appearances, and was widely regarded as one of the best in the NFL. Who's the other player in question?

    a. Jahleel Addae
    b. Brandon Dunn
    c. Laremy Tunsil
    d. Carlos Watkins

14. Eric Winston anchored the right side of the Houston offensive line from 2006 to 2011. For which coach's running game was he a key component?

    a. Dom Capers
    b. Gary Kubiak
    c. Bill O'Brien
    d. Wade Phillips

15. Chester Pitts started every game on the Texans' offensive line from 2002 to 2008. He was considered as dependable as a Houston summer storm or traffic on ___. Which Houston highway?

    a. I-10
    b. I-45
    c. 290
    d. Hardy Toll Road

16. Wade Smith was the first offensive lineman ever to score a touchdown for the Houston franchise. Who were the sorry opponents on that day in 2011?

a. Baltimore Ravens

b. Cincinnati Bengals

c. Dallas Cowboys

d. Denver Broncos

17. Off the field, Smith gave back (and still gives back) to the community through the Wade Smith Foundation, reading programs, and anti-bullying campaigns. Which team did Smith move to after Houston?

a. Buffalo

b. Miami

c. New England

d. Philadelphia

18. Tytus Howard was drafted by the Houston Texans in the 1st round (23rd overall) of the 2019 NFL Draft. He was the first player from his university ever to be picked in the 1st round. Which university was it?

a. Alabama A&M

b. Alabama State

c. Troy University

d. University of North Alabama

19. When massive Max Scharping participated in the 2019 NFL Scouting Combine, he completed 24 reps on the bench press.

a. True

b. False

20. Despite Nick Martin signing a three-year, $33 million contract extension, with $18.5 million guaranteed by the Texans, he was released in 2021. He played for many years, including starting side by side for the Notre Dame Fighting Irish, with his brother. What was his brother's name?

   a. Sidney
   b. Solomon
   c. Zack
   d. Zeke

QUIZ ANSWERS

1. C – 2017

2. A – Awareness

3. D – Wreaking havoc

4. C – Ninja Assassin

5. D – Bryon Leftwich

6. B – 2005

7. C – 19

8. A – True

9. C – 21

10. D – Tucson, Arizona

11. B – 8

12. D – Offensive

13. C – Laremy Tunsil

14. B – Gary Kubiak

15. C – 290

16. A – Baltimore Ravens

17. D – Philadelphia

18. B – Alabama State

19. B – False (He completed 27 reps.)

20. C – Zack

DID YOU KNOW?

1. In 2014, J.J. Watt became the first player in NFL history to record two 20+ sack seasons in a career. In addition, he holds Houston's franchise records for both sacks and forced fumbles.

2. While preparing himself for the 2014 NFL Draft, Jadeveon Clowney basked in praise: "Clowney's a rare talent, basically to the defensive end spot what Andrew Luck and RG3 were to the quarterback position," claimed ESPN analyst Mel Kiper Jr. "These type of prospects just don't come along very often." NFL Media analyst Bucky Brooks said Clowney was a "meaner, nastier version of Julius Peppers."

3. In 2013, Antonio Smith got a bit carried away and was suspended for Week 1 after a preseason incident when he removed Miami Dolphins lineman Richie Incognito's helmet and swung it at him.

4. Before the Texans-Colts game in 2007, Indianapolis coach Tony Dungy compared Mario Williams to Colts Pro Bowl defensive end Dwight Freeney. Mario's first sack of the season, when he corralled Peyton Manning, came soon after.

5. Shaun Cody was head coach Pete Carroll's first blue-chip recruit at USC, which in turn attracted other talented

players, eventually leading to the dominance by the Trojans in the early 2000s.

6. Travis Johnson racked up 104 tackles, including 32 for losses, and 17 sacks as a senior for the Notre Dame Knights of Sherman Oaks (CA), while setting school records for career sacks (61), tackles for loss (77), forced fumbles (14), and blocked punts (5).

7. Amobi Okoye was named Defensive Rookie of the Month in September 2007, when he led the AFC with four sacks. He was the youngest player ever to receive the award, at age 19.

8. Vince Wilfork started all 16 games for Houston in 2015 at the nose tackle position and made 22 tackles. In two seasons for the Texans, he totaled 43 tackles, helping the team win back-to-back AFC South titles.

9. On November 27, 2011, Connor Barwin had a career-best 10 tackles and set a team record for sacks in a game with four in Houston's 20-13 victory over the Jaguars at EverBank Field.

10. Unfortunately, Duane Brown's time in Houston came to a stormy end after former owner Bob McNair made one of the worst comments in sports history, referring to the players as "inmates."

CHAPTER 7:

NO AIR ZONE

QUIZ TIME!

1. The Texans selected Justin Reid in the 3rd round (the 68th overall pick) of the 2018 NFL Draft. Reid was the fifth safety drafted in 2018. He fell unexpectedly from the 1st or 2nd round to the 3rd and was then ranked among the top _____ of the 2018 Draft. What's missing?

   a. Busts
   b. Defenders
   c. Secret agents
   d. Steals

2. Reid's special stop of a Jaguar in the 2019 Week 2 game sealed the win and showed what a special talent Justin is. Who was the unlucky Jag that bore the brunt of the Reid hit?

   a. Leonard Fournette
   b. Rashad Green
   c. Devine Ozigbo
   d. Thomas Rawls

3. Bernard Pollard's hit on New England's Tom Brady ended the latter's season abruptly in 2008 and earned the former a unique nickname. What was it?

   a. The Brady Blaster
   b. The New England Neutralizer
   c. The Patriot Killer
   d. The Patriot Pulverizer

4. Despite "only" starring at the Division II level in college, Danieal Manning became one of the Texans' all-time best defensive backs. Which university did he attend?

   a. Abilene Christian
   b. Baylor
   c. Southern Methodist
   d. St. Mary's

5. Andre Hal blossomed as a Houston safety. What position did he start at as a Texan in 2014?

   a. Cornerback
   b. Linebacker
   c. Quarterback
   d. Wide receiver

6. Despite C.C. Brown's effectiveness and tenacity as a Texans defender, he was accused of a crime while in Houston. What did he allegedly do?

   a. Defraud an NFL players' health care plan
   b. Miss practices due to various bogus excuses
   c. Park his car for free in a restricted zone
   d. Steal Houston jerseys for resale

7. Playing for the Alabama Crimson Tide starting in 2007, in which year did safety Kareem Jackson win All-American honors?

   a. Freshman
   b. Sophomore
   c. Junior
   d. Senior

8. Picked by Houston in 2010, Jackson was the second cornerback taken overall in the NFL Draft. Who was the first that year?

   a. Sam Bradford, Oklahoma
   b. Brandon Graham, Michigan
   c. Joe Haden, Florida
   d. C.J. Spiller, Clemson

9. Safety Quintin Demps had two stints batting down passes in Houston. Which UFL team did he also play for briefly?

   a. Florida Tuskers
   b. Hartford Colonials
   c. New York Sentinels
   d. Omaha Nighthawks

10. After defending Mississippi State, safety Eric Brown was a member of Houston's inaugural season roster in 2002. He also won a Super Bowl with the Broncos, who beat the Falcons at the end of the 1998 campaign.

    a. True
    b. False

11. Marcus Coleman played defensive back for Houston, Dallas, and the New York Jets. Which Indoor Football League team was he named head coach of in 2018?

    a. Green Bay Blizzard

    b. Iowa Barnstormers

    c. Tucson Sugar Skulls

    d. West Texas Warbirds

12. Troy Nolan attended El Camino Real High School in Woodland Hills, California. In which of the following sports did he NOT letter?

    a. Baseball

    b. Basketball

    c. Soccer

    d. Track and field

13. During a preseason game against the Minnesota Vikings on August 31, 2009, Eugene Wilson fell victim to an illegal block thrown by Brett Favre. What kind of block was it called?

    a. Crackback

    b. No-look

    c. Spearing

    d. Underhanded

14. Elbert Mack played cornerback for Houston in 2013 and 2014. Which team did he suit up for in the China Arena Football League (CAFL) starting in 2018?

    a. Beijing Lions

    b. Qingdao Clipper

c. Shanghai Skywalkers

d. Wuhan Gators

15. Before being converted to defensive back, Brian Russell handled the quarterbacking duties. In fact, he was the first freshman ever to start a game in 1996 at that position for an Ivy League school. Which was it?

a. Cornell

b. Dartmouth

c. Penn

d. Princeton

16. Russell's last NFL game was played on January 3, 2010, when he helped Houston secure their first winning season by beating the New England Patriots. Where was that game played?

a. Barnett Sports Complex

b. Minute Maid Park

c. Reliant Stadium

d. The Ballpark

17. Defensive back Kendrick Lewis led the Texans in tackles in 2014. How many times did he stuff opponents that season?

a. 65

b. 76

c. 84

d. 97

18. In addition to the Texans in 2013-14, cornerback Josh Victorian played with 12 other pro football teams. Which of the following was NOT one of them?

    a. Baltimore Ravens
    b. Los Angeles KISS
    c. New Orleans Voodoo
    d. Washington Valor

19. Michael Boulware saw time for the Texans in 2007. He's better known for his pickoff in Super Bowl XL, which helped the Seahawks, albeit in a losing effort. Which quarterback served up the interception that day?

    a. Tom Brady
    b. Drew Brees
    c. Carson Palmer
    d. Ben Roethlisberger

20. On October 30, 2016, Johnson Bademosi recorded his first interception in the league against the Texans, picking off Brock Osweiler in a 20-13 loss. Johnson later played with Houston in 2018.

    a. True
    b. False

QUIZ ANSWERS

1. D – Steals

2. A – Leonard Fournette

3. C – The Patriot Killer

4. A – Abilene Christian

5. A – Cornerback

6. A – Defraud an NFL players' health care plan

7. A – Freshman

8. C – Joe Haden, Florida

9. B – Hartford Colonials

10. A – True

11. C – Tucson Sugar Skulls

12. A – Baseball

13. A – Crackback

14. B – Qingdao Clipper

15. C – Penn

16. C – Reliant Stadium

17. C – 84

18. A – Baltimore Ravens

19. D – Ben Roethlisberger

20. A – True

DID YOU KNOW?

1. Justin Reid is already considered one of the greatest safeties in franchise history. On October 7, 2018, in Week 5 against the Dallas Cowboys, he recorded his first career interception off of Dak Prescott in a 19-16 win.

2. Bernard Pollard was "one of the hardest-hitting safeties of the 21st century." He went on to become the Chiefs' top tackler with 98 total in 2008.

3. Danieal Manning made his mark in 2011 when he intercepted Tennessee quarterback Matt Hasselbeck, returning it 55 yards for a touchdown. During his 3.5 years in Houston, Manning had 206 combined tackles, 156 solo tackles, four tackles for a loss, four interceptions, three forced fumbles, two fumble recoveries, and 26 passes defensed.

4. On June 6, 2018, only a year after he signed a deserved contract extension, Andre Hal was diagnosed with Hodgkin's Lymphoma and put on the reserve/non-football injury list. Hal's career seemed over just when it was starting to take off. However, Hal triumphed over cancer and returned to the field in Week 7 against Jacksonville.

5. During his time in Houston's "battle red" uniforms from 2005 to 2009, C.C. Brown started 47 games, pitched in with 256 combined tackles, 197 solo tackles, five tackles for loss, three interceptions, and four fumble recoveries.

6. On November 28, 2010, Glover Quin showed his worth to Texan fans: He recorded a career-high four pass deflections, made four combined tackles, and intercepted three passes by quarterback Rusty Smith in the Texans' 20-0 win against Tennessee in Week 14.

7. In Week 4 of the 2010 NFL season, safety Troy Nolan made his first career and regular-season appearance against the Oakland Raiders. He snagged two interceptions, and the second was the game-winner.

8. Josh Aubrey is a homegrown product, having played high school ball for Tyler Lee in Texas and then collegiately for the Stephen F. Austin State University Lumberjacks, before suiting up for the Browns, Seahawks, Texans, and Titans.

9. Safety Tashaun Gipson helped the Texans celebrate a big win in Week 5 of 2019 against the Atlanta Falcons, recording a 79-yard pick-six off Matt Ryan in the 53-32 victory.

10. Since scoring his first career touchdown on December 21, 2003, a 95-yard interception return off of the Titans' Steve McNair, Marlon McCree went on to become the assistant defensive backs coach for the Jaguars in 2012.

CHAPTER 8:

SHINING THE BUSTS

QUIZ TIME!

1. Defensive end J.J. Watt is Houston's most decorated player. How many times was he named the Associated Press Defensive Player of the Year?

    a. 2

    b. 3

    c. 4

    d. 6

2. Who was the first Texans player ever to receive an All-Pro First Team selection, in 2005?

    a. Arian Foster

    b. Andre Johnson

    c. Jerome Mathis

    d. DeMeco Ryans

3. Houston receiver Andre Johnson was named to two consecutive AP All-Pro First Team squads in 2008 and 2009, after being a Second Team selection in 2006.

a. True

b. False

4. Another Houston player besides Arian Foster was picked for the AP First Team All-Pro squad in 2010: Vonta Leach. What was his position?

a. Fullback

b. Punt returner

c. Tight end

d. Wide receiver

5. Linebacker DeMeco Ryans was named the AP Rookie of the Year in what year?

a. 2000

b. 2003

c. 2006

d. 2008

6. In Houston's inaugural season of 2002, two Texans made it to the Pro Bowl. Besides cornerback Aaron Glenn, who was the other?

a. Jarod Baxter, fullback

b. David Carr, quarterback

c. Gary Walker, defensive tackle

d. Jonathan Wells, running back

7. In which of the following years did the Texans have more players (9) in the Pro Bowl than any other?

a. 2004

b. 2007

c. 2009

d. 2012

8. Which of the following Texans was honored with more Pro Bowl selections (7) than any other?

   a. DeAndre Hopkins

   b. Andre Johnson

   c. Matt Schaub

   d. J.J. Watt

9. When Texans quarterback Matt Schaub copped the Pro Bowl MVP in 2010, the attendance was reported to be 70,697—the most for a Pro Bowl since 1959, when the game was played in Los Angeles. Where was the 2010 contest?

   a. Dallas

   b. Miami

   c. Phoenix

   d. Honolulu

10. Texans running back Domanick Davis was elected the Pepsi NFL Rookie of the Year for his outstanding 2003 season. Who voted him in?

    a. Coaches

    b. Fans

    c. Fellow players

    d. Writers

11. Brian Cushing played linebacker for the Texans from 2009 to 2017, became the franchise's all-time leading tackler,

and was voted team MVP in 2011. What kind of assistant coach did he become after his playing days?

a. College scouting
b. Defensive coordinator
c. Game management
d. Strength and conditioning

12. Houston's DeMeco Ryans was named Defensive Rookie of the Year in 2007. He later became the defensive coordinator for a top NFL franchise. Which one?

a. Chicago Bears
b. Indianapolis Colts
c. San Francisco 49ers
d. Seattle Seahawks

13. Cornerback William Dunta Robinson was voted by teammates as Houston's rookie of the year in 2004. He grew up in the shadows of the University of Georgia but decided to commit to another college. Which one?

a. Clemson
b. Nebraska
c. North Carolina
d. South Carolina

14. Fred Bennett also played cornerback as a Texan and was voted rookie of the year by his peers in 2007. After his NFL days were done, what was the first Canadian team he played for?

a. Calgary Stampeders
b. Montreal Alouettes

c. Saskatchewan Roughriders

d. Toronto Argonauts

15. Defender Earl Mitchell was heralded by Houston teammates as the team's best rookie in 2010. He later came out of retirement, signed with the 49ers in January 2020, and reached Super Bowl LIV with San Fran, but lost to the Chiefs, 31-20. Mitchell recorded one tackle and 0.5 sacks in the Super Bowl but missed his elusive ring.

a. True

b. False

16. The Houston team gives an annual award in the name of Mark Bruener. Which of the following aspects is NOT considered vital to winning this award?

a. Commitment

b. Outstanding leadership

c. Salary expectations

d. Work ethic

17. Who was the first Texan to be awarded the Ed Block Courage Award, in 2002, for serving as a source of courage and inspiration?

a. Jason Bell

b. Aaron Glenn

c. Seth Payne

d. Kailee Wong

18. Though Jabar Gaffney was also given the Ed Block Courage Award, his stint with the team was disrupted by

his frequent inconsistent play which led to his benching in favor of veteran receivers. He wasn't re-signed by Houston after his rookie year.

a. True
b. False

19. Honored by his 2014 Houston teammates, offensive tackle David Quessenberry had previously been team captain and a Burlsworth Trophy finalist for the best non-scholarship NCAA-FBS player. Which university did he play for?

a. San Diego State
b. San Jose State
c. UCLA
d. USC

20. When did Houston finally win its first AFC South division championship?

a. 2007
b. 2009
c. 2011
d. 2013

QUIZ ANSWERS

1. B – 3

2. C – Jerome Mathis

3. A – True

4. A – Fullback

5. C – 2006

6. C – Gary Walker, defensive tackle

7. D – 2012

8. B – Andre Johnson

9. B – Miami

10. B – Fans

11. D – Strength and conditioning

12. C – San Francisco 49ers

13. D – South Carolina

14. A – Calgary Stampeders

15. A – True

16. C – Salary expectations

17. A – Jason Bell

18. A – True

19. B – San Jose State

20. C – 2011

DID YOU KNOW?

1. Many experts believed Schaub's 2009 season was fine enough to get him to the Pro Bowl without being selected as an alternate. Houston's quarterback threw for an NFL-best 4,770 yards with 29 touchdowns and 15 interceptions for the 9-7 Texans.

2. Six-year veteran Schaub completed 13 of 17 passes (76.5%) for 189 yards and two touchdowns while leading the AFC to a 41-34 win in the 2010 Pro Bowl. His performance netted him the game's Most Valuable Player award. "It's a game you watch growing up as a kid and wonder if you could ever be in," Schaub told reporters later. "To actually be a part of it is incredible."

3. Since he rushed for more than 1,000 yards in each of his first two seasons, Domanick Davis received a contract extension before the start of the 2005 campaign. Before the extension, Davis was due to make $385,000 that year. The extension assured a payout of $22 million over the life of the deal, with $8 million in guaranteed money.

4. Award-winning linebacker Brian Cushing returned a botched onside kick attempt by Notre Dame at the Los Angeles Memorial Coliseum for a late fourth-quarter touchdown on November 25, 2006. He was named the 2007 Rose Bowl MVP soon after.

5. Houston runner Steve Slaton was declared the 2006 Nokia Sugar Bowl MVP after rushing for 204 yards on 26 carries and scoring three touchdowns in a 38-35 win for his West Virginia University team over Georgia. He was then named Houston rookie of the year in 2008 by fellow players.

6. The centerpiece of a young line for the Georgia Bulldogs, Ben Jones protected quarterback Matthew Stafford, who threw for 3,459 yards (second most in school history) and 25 touchdowns (a single-season record), while clearing the way for runner Knowshon Moreno (1,400 rushing yards). As a senior in 2011, Jones was named an ESPN All-American.

7. The Spirit of the Bull Award is given annually by the team to a Texans player who best exemplifies a commitment to excellence, both on and off the field, as well as for charitable work in the Houston community. Some winners have been DeMeco Ryans, Andre Johnson, Matt Schaub, and J.J. Watt.

8. In 2009, the Spirit of the Bull Award was renamed to honor tight end Mark Bruener, who won the award for four straight years from 2005 to 2008.

9. Yet another Ed Block Courage Award winner, Anthony Weaver, had a six-year playing career and then became a successful coach. In 2016, Weaver was hired by Houston as their defensive line coach under head coach Bill O'Brien. In January of 2020, Weaver was promoted to defensive coordinator and defensive line coach.

10. In 2007, Joel Dreessen scored his first and Houston's only touchdown in a 35-10 loss to San Diego. He was named Houston's top offensive player despite having only one reception. Dreessen re-signed with the Texans in 2009 for a reported three-year, $3.6 million deal.

CHAPTER 9:

DRAFT DAY

QUIZ TIME!

1. Which player was drafted just before J.J. Watt (at 10th overall in 2011), who had an anemic career, but ended up with something Watt doesn't have: a Super Bowl ring (as Tom Brady's backup in Tampa Bay)?

   a. Andy Dalton
   b. Joe Flacco
   c. Blaine Gabbert
   d. Cam Newton

2. Watt skipped his senior season as a Wisconsin Badger to enter the 2011 NFL Draft. He was a top performer in all the scouting combine categories before the draft, except one. Which one was too tough for J.J.?

   a. Bench press
   b. Broad jump
   c. 40-yard dash
   d. Three-cone drill

3. While Deshaun Watson was taken 12th overall in 2017, Patrick Mahomes (already the owner of a league MVP and Super Bowl ring) was taken 10th. How many quarterbacks were picked that year?

   a. 8
   b. 10
   c. 12
   d. 15

4. Watson was rated as the top quarterback available in the 2017 Draft by *Sports Illustrated*, *Pro Football Focus*, and ESPN. He was ranked the second-best quarterback by NFLDraftScout.com.

   a. True
   b. False

5. Andre Johnson was picked 3rd overall by Houston in 2003. Besides being inducted into the Texas Sports Hall of Fame in 2019, which elite group was Johnson the inaugural member of in 2017?

   a. Dallas Press Club Honor Roll
   b. Houston Sports Hall of Fame
   c. Texans Ring of Honor
   d. University of Houston Hall of Honor

6. Before joining Houston as the 27th overall pick in 2013, DeAndre Hopkins had private workouts with a number of teams. Which of the following did he NOT audition for privately?

a. Carolina

b. Dallas

c. St. Louis

d. Tennessee

7. Duane Brown (selected 26th overall by Houston) was only the second Virginia Tech offensive lineman ever drafted in the 1st round of an NFL Draft. Who was the first?

a. Kam Chancellor

b. Eugene Chung

c. DeAngelo Hall

d. Michael Vick

8. Brown became the first Houston rookie lineman to start all 16 games since another terrific Texan did it in 2002. Who is the man in question?

a. Brandon Brooks

b. Chester Pitts

c. Jimmy Smith

d. Laremy Tunsil

9. Some pundits believe that Houston shouldn't have taken David Carr with the first pick in 2002, but rather with the 2nd overall pick. Who was this future Hall-of-Famer?

a. Joey Harrington

b. Quentin Jammer

c. Julius Peppers

d. Ryan Sims

10. The 41st overall pick in the 2003 Draft was supposed to pair with David Carr, yet he never caught a pass in the NFL. Who was this masked man?

   a. Ryan Hoag
   b. Dan Klecko
   c. Bennie Joppru
   d. Seth Wand

11. The Texans took Tony Hollings in the 2nd round of the 2003 Supplemental Draft. How many yards did he gain in three Houston years?

   a. 119
   b. 149
   c. 235
   d. 410

12. In 2007, Houston passed on the likes of Marshawn Lynch and Patrick Willis to select Amobi Okoye. This was the first pick ever by a particular general manager for the Texans. Who was he?

   a. Charley Casserly
   b. Brian Gaine
   c. Bill O'Brien
   d. Rick Smith

13. Brandon Harris was grabbed by the Texans in 2011 with the 60th overall pick but was cut less than three years later. What edition of the Grey Cup did he win with the Toronto Argonauts in 2017?

a. 57th

b. 85th

c. 99th

d. 105th

14. Sam Montgomery was drafted by the Texans in 2013 and released the same year, along with two other players, for "unspecified violations of team rules" on a road trip. Who was the game against?

    a. Jacksonville

    b. Kansas City

    c. Miami

    d. Minnesota

15. Louis Nix was drafted by Houston in the 3rd round (83rd overall) of the 2014 NFL Draft. On May 16, 2014, he signed a $2.85 million contract with the team, including a signing bonus of $575,252. Then he underwent four knee surgeries by September and never played again in Houston.

    a. True

    b. False

16. Analysts projected Kevin Johnson would be a 1st round draft choice coming out of Wake Forest. He was ranked the second-best cornerback in the land by NFLDraftScout.com in 2015. How many other cornerbacks were available in that year's draft?

    a. 55

    b. 126

c. 187

d. 212

17. Jaelen Strong was picked 70th overall in 2015. He had mild success as a rookie against the Colts but frequent trips to the Bill O'Brien _____ doomed him. What's missing?

   a. Cuckoo's nest

   b. Doghouse

   c. Farmhouse

   d. Kennel

18. Before being drafted by the Texans, Whitney Mercilus won the 2011 Ted Hendricks Award, 2011 Bill Willis Award, and 2011 CFPA Defensive Performer of the Year, in addition to being a unanimous First Team All-American. Who was his head coach at Illinois?

   a. Montee Ball

   b. Rex Burkhead

   c. Russell Wilson

   d. Ron Zook

19. Which of the following cornerbacks was Kareem Jackson NOT ranked behind by scouting combines entering the 2010 Draft?

   a. Joe Haden

   b. Johnathan Joseph

   c. Devin McCourty

   d. Kyle Wilson

20. Despite being scooped up by Houston with the 16th overall pick in 2005, Travis Johnson saw limited action due to injuries. Which team did he hook up with after Houston?

   a. Atlanta
   b. Indianapolis
   c. San Diego
   d. San Francisco

QUIZ ANSWERS

1. C – Blaine Gabbert

2. C – 40-yard dash

3. B – 10

4. A – True

5. C – Texans Ring of Honor

6. D – Tennessee

7. B – Eugene Chung

8. B – Chester Pitts

9. C – Julius Peppers

10. C – Bennie Joppru

11. B – 149 (on 49 carries)

12. D – Rick Smith

13. D – 105th

14. B – Kansas City

15. B – False (Nix underwent three knee surgeries.)

16. D – 212

17. B – Doghouse

18. D – Ron Zook

19. B – Jonathan Joseph

20. C – San Diego

DID YOU KNOW?

1. The Texans have drafted 12 running backs in their 18-year history but have never selected one in the 1st round.

2. Among undrafted running backs, Texan Arian Foster trails only Joe Perry and Priest Holmes in career rushing yards. His 1,616 yards from 2010 is the most in a single season by an undrafted player.

3. Seth Payne was selected by the Texans in the 2002 Expansion Draft, along with Jaguars teammates Tony Boselli and Gary Walker. The move allowed Jacksonville to get under the salary cap but was still surprising given that the Texans and Jaguars were in the same division.

4. Recognizing Ben Tate's value at the 58th overall pick in 2010, the Texans traded up aggressively to draft him, which was the only time in team history that the Texans drafted a running back earlier than the 3rd round.

5. DeAndre Hopkins was the second wide receiver in franchise history to be drafted in the 1st round. Andre Johnson was the first, selected 3rd overall in 2003. Also, it was just the second time in a decade that Houston selected an offensive player (The other was left tackle Duane Brown.) in the 1st round.

6. In the 2012 Draft, in which Deshaun Watson was selected, player selections were made in an outdoor theater built on

the "Rocky Steps" in Philadelphia, marking the first time an entire NFL Draft was held outdoors. The draft was also the most attended in history, with more than 250,000 people present.

7. Andre Johnson is considered the best player in franchise history who has already retired. Debatably, he was the first true fan favorite. Johnson was the 3rd overall pick in the 2003 Draft and spent 12 years with the team.

8. Head coach Gary Kubiak said this upon the conclusion of the 2012 Draft: "I just want to say I think Rick (Smith) and the scouts did a tremendous job. Obviously, the coaches have done their work over the course of the last couple of months. It's just nice to see things come together. I feel very good about our draft class, not only adding quality talent to our football team but a lot of passion."

9. GM Rick Smith clarified the 2012 choice of kicker Randy Bullock in the draft: "First of all, he's a very talented young man. That's apparent, and he has a very strong leg. He's had some success kicking at A&M, again, big school, big competition. I like his mental makeup."

10. Xavier Su'a-Filo was selected by Houston with the first pick in the 2nd round (33rd overall) of the 2014 NFL Draft. He became the highest selected UCLA Bruins offensive lineman since Jonathan Ogden in 1996.

CHAPTER 10:

LET'S MAKE A DEAL!

QUIZ TIME!

1. Disappointment with Brock Osweiler and Tom Savage made Houston trade to move up in the 2017 NFL Draft to secure Deshaun Watson. What team did they deal with?

    a. Chicago
    b. Cleveland
    c. Denver
    d. Green Bay

2. In his lone season as a Texan, Brock Osweiler's franchise-record number of interceptions was one reason Houston unloaded him. How many picks did he offer up in 2016?

    a. 13
    b. 16
    c. 20
    d. 24

3. The exchange allowed Cleveland to absorb some of Osweiler's cap from Houston in exchange for draft

picks—one of the first trades of its kind. In the end, Houston used the money saved in this swap to re-sign cornerback Johnathan Joseph and sign free agent safety Tyrann Mathieu.

   a. True
   b. False

4. Former Virginia Cavalier Matt Schaub stayed in Texas for seven seasons until 2013 and was then traded to a team on the West Coast in exchange for a 2014 6th round draft pick. Which team?

   a. San Diego
   b. San Francisco
   c. Seattle
   d. Oakland

5. How many trades did Houston make before its inaugural campaign even began in 2002?

   a. 8
   b. 6
   c. 5
   d. 3

6. After offensive sparkplug DeAndre Hopkins was sent packing to Arizona in 2020, what were the ripple effects felt in Houston?

   a. Bill O'Brien was fired.
   b. Hopkins thrived in Phoenix.
   c. Houston started the season 0-4.
   d. All of the above

7. In 2017, the Seahawks received Duane Brown and a 2018 5th round draft pick, and the Texans raked in a 3rd round pick in 2018 and a 2nd round pick in 2019. Initially, Seattle cornerback Jeremy Lane was also on his way to Houston as part of the deal, but he failed a physical.

   a. True
   b. False

8. Although it hurt to see a specific Houston defensive leader in another uniform, the Texans obtained excellent value from the trade. Who was the Texan traded in 2012?

   a. Brian Cushing
   b. Ben Jones
   c. DeMeco Ryans
   d. Zach Thomas

9. When Houston traded for Demaryius Thomas in 2018, he stood as the second leading receiver in the history of his previous team. Which franchise was it?

   a. Dallas
   b. Denver
   c. Philadelphia
   d. Pittsburgh

10. Before being shipped to Houston, Jay Foreman didn't take the news well that a replacement had been found for him at weakside linebacker in Buffalo. Who was the Bills' coach that made that call?

   a. Joe Collier
   b. Mike Mularkey

c. Wade Phillips

d. Gregg Williams

11. For a mere 6ᵗʰ round pick back in 2008, the Texans gained a future two-time Pro Bowl center. Who was he?

a. Mike Flanagan

b. Chris Myers

c. Chester Pitts

d. Eric Winston

12. A 2015 draft pick from New England allowed Houston to peg D.J. Reader. Who was then relied on to develop Reader into a top nose tackle?

a. Chris Clark

b. Kendall Lamm

c. Robaire Smith

d. Vince Wilfork

13. Mid- or late-round picks are hard to predict. Gems are hard to come by after a hundred or so players are sifted through—but that's why they're called gems. D.J. Reader, 6ᵗʰ round selection, is considered one such player.

a. True

b. False

14. In exchange for DeAndre Hopkins, the Texans received a running back who was largely inconsistent since 2016 and a 2ⁿᵈ round pick. Who was that running back?

a. Jonathan Grimes

b. Kenny Hilliard

c. Akeem Hunt

d. David Johnson

15. The Texans needed a left tackle to guard their most valuable player, Watson, ever since they traded Duane Brown in 2017. Who did they trade for just before the season to try to fill the need?

a. Chris Clark

b. Nick Martin

c. Kenny Stills

d. Laremy Tunsil

16. Before being traded to the Seahawks in 2019, Jadeveon Clowney nixed a trade to another team he thought was "tanking." Which team?

a. Cincinnati

b. Jacksonville

c. Miami

d. Tampa Bay

17. Duke Johnson made it known he was unhappy in Cleveland in 2019 and was traded to Houston for what turned into a future 3rd round pick. How many yards per catch had the dual threat averaged in his career?

a. 7.2

b. 9.2

c. 11.4

d. 14.7

18. When Lamar Miller was lost for the season early in 2019, the Texans decided to offload a promising youngster for a veteran rusher, Kansas City's Carlos Hyde. Who did Houston deal away?

    a. Ross Blacklock
    b. Charles Omenihu
    c. Martinas Rankin
    d. John Reid

19. Houston took a chance by trading for receiver Brandin Cooks because he suffered two concussions in a short period. Whose high hit knocked Cooks out of Super Bowl LII while he was with the Patriots?

    a. Trey Burton
    b. Fletcher Cox
    c. Brandon Graham
    d. Malcolm Jenkins

20. When Houston acquired quarterback Ryan Mallett from New England in 2014, who was he brought in to replace?

    a. Ryan Fitzpatrick
    b. Case Keenum
    c. Brock Osweiler
    d. Tom Savage

QUIZ ANSWERS

1. B – Cleveland

2. B – 16

3. A – True

4. D – Oakland

5. C – 5

6. D – All of the above

7. A – True

8. C – DeMeco Ryans

9. B – Denver

10. D – Gregg Williams

11. B – Chris Myers

12. D – Vince Wilfork

13. A – True

14. D – David Johnson

15. D – Laremy Tunsil

16. C – Miami

17. B – 9.2

18. C – Martinas Rankin

19. D – Malcolm Jenkins

20. A – Ryan Fitzpatrick

DID YOU KNOW?

1. In terms of investment, the Texans came up a bit short on Jason Babin. Houston traded 2nd, 3rd, 4th, and 5th round picks to get Babin, who had 13 sacks in three seasons, and got a 5th round pick back.

2. Deemed by some as "one of the worst trades in league history," Houston elicited visceral reactions from the public when the front office sent All-Pro wide receiver DeAndre Hopkins to Arizona in 2020.

3. In 2007, the front office decided to ditch quarterback David Carr and aimed for Matt Schaub, who was the perennial backup quarterback to Michael Vick with the Atlanta Falcons.

4. Schaub's agent, Joby Branion, summed up his client's trade: "I dealt with [Texans General Manager] Rick Smith on Ahman Green a couple of weeks ago. That gave us a great deal of comfort heading into these discussions believing we could get something done and we did."

5. Houston's scouting department did an amazing job finding a gem in linebacker Bernardrick McKinney in a shallow 2015 NFL Draft. But first, the front office needed to secure a trade with the Browns in order for them to land a higher draft pick.

6. The fifth trade Houston swung before their first season in 2002 was consummated to acquire linebacker Jay Foreman from the Buffalo Bills in exchange for running back Charlie Rogers.

7. A University of Nebraska-Lincoln product, Foreman spent his best seasons with Houston, becoming the leading tackler in the franchise's debut season. He established himself as the team's second and third leader in tackles over the next two seasons, respectively.

8. Here's the Hopkins swap as seen from the Arizona side: "The earth-shattering trade that went down this past offseason leads off this list, as the Houston Texans and head coach/general manager hybrid that is Bill O'Brien was not all that keen (apparently) on keeping what was easily the best player on his team in wide receiver DeAndre Hopkins."

9. "The transaction left many scratching their heads in an attempt to understand (a) why the Texans would trade arguably their best offensive playmaker, and (b) why the return seemed so low for one of the best receivers in the league," a *Forbes* article continued on December 3, 2020.

10. In the 2015 Draft, the Texans and Browns once again got very involved. Houston traded 2nd, 4th, and 6th round picks to Cleveland for an earlier 2nd and 7th round pick. The Texans picked linebacker Benardrick McKinney with the 2nd round pick and traded the 7th round selection.

CHAPTER 11:

WRITING THE RECORD BOOK

QUIZ TIME!

1. In which year did the Houston franchise manage the most home wins (7) in its short history?

    a. 2010
    b. 2013
    c. 2016
    d. 2019

2. The Texans amassed a record number of points in one particularly productive season, 2012. How many points did Houston pile up that year?

    a. 385
    b. 416
    c. 477
    d. 520

3. One sorry rival allowed Houston to rack up a record number of points in a single game on October 1, 2017, in

what turned out to be a 57-14 Texans victory. Who was the opponent?

a. Carolina
b. Indianapolis
c. Jacksonville
d. Tennessee

4. Houston's biggest comeback on record occurred against San Diego on September 9, 2013, when the team roared back to snag an improbable 31-28 win. How many points were the Texans behind at one point in the game?

a. 28
b. 24
c. 21
d. 18

5. Which Houston player shares the record for most consecutive starts and most games played in franchise history, with 171?

a. Jahleel Addae
b. Breno Giacomini
c. Andre Johnson
d. Jon Weeks

6. One Houston quarterback stood above the rest in terms of the highest completion percentage in franchise history, with 65.6%. Who was he?

a. Ryan Finley
b. Ryan Fitzpatrick

c. Sage Rosenfels

d. Matt Schaub

7. Arian Foster holds practically every conceivable rushing record for the Texans, including attempts, total yards, touchdowns, and number of games with 100 yards or more gained. However, which Houston runner has the highest per-carry yards average at 4.7?

a. Justin Forsett

b. Mark Ingram Jr.

c. Lamar Miller

d. Ben Tate

8. Arian Foster was missed completely in the 2009 NFL Draft but hitched a ride with the Texans as an undrafted free agent. Though he came into the NFL with a big chip on his shoulder, he left as one of the top NFL running backs from the early 2010s. In 2010, he led the league with 1,616 rushing yards and 16 touchdowns, as well as 393 touches and 2,220 total offensive yards.

a. True

b. False

9. Similar to Foster's running, Andre Johnson holds almost every imaginable receiving record, including number of receptions, total yards in the air, receiving touchdowns, and receiving yards per game. One other pass catcher owns a Houston record: most receiving yards on average per reception at 16.4. Who is he?

a. Owen Daniels

b. André Davis

c. DeAndre Hopkins

d. Kevin Walter

10. In the history of the Houston franchise, which player has scored the greatest number of points, with 767?

a. Kris Brown

b. Ka'imi Fairbairn

c. Arian Foster

d. Andre Johnson

11. Besides defending a record number of passes (117) as a Texan, how many pass interception return yards did Johnathan Joseph rack up in his career to lead all Houston defenders?

a. 320

b. 385

c. 410

d. 552

12. J.J. Watt sure knew how to jar the ball loose from unwary opponents. What was the record number of fumbles he caused, and what is his record for fumbles recovered that he established at Houston?

a. 18/13

b. 23/15

c. 27/18

d. 35/21

13. J.J. Moses handled every kind of kick return for Houston, as well as Arizona and Green Bay. During his career, he was listed as the shortest active NFL player. What was his actual height?

    a. 5'4" (162.5 cm)
    b. 5'6" (167.6 cm)
    c. 5'7" (170 cm)
    d. 5'9" (175 cm)

14. Jerome Mathis holds the Houston record for average yards gained on kickoff returns at 28.5. With which player did he tie for the most kickoff returns for touchdowns, with three?

    a. André Davis
    b. Will Fuller V
    c. Jacoby Jones
    d. J.J. Moses

15. Return specialist Jacoby Jones set several punt return records while in Houston from 2007 to 2011, including punt return yards (1,820) and touchdowns (3). He's arguably more famous for his kickoff return for a touchdown as a member of the Baltimore Ravens against the San Francisco 49ers in Super Bowl XLVII, which turned out to be the longest play in Super Bowl history. How many yards did he gallop?

    a. 110
    b. 108
    c. 106
    d. 103

16. In the 2016 season, receiver and return dynamo Will Vincent Fuller V became the first Texan ever to catch a touchdown pass and return a punt for a touchdown, a 67-yard return, in the same game. Who was the foe that day?

    a. Carolina
    b. Indianapolis
    c. Jacksonville
    d. Tennessee

17. Neil Rackers replaced kicker Kris Brown in 2010 and established a Houston record for field goal percentage (86.8%). After his retirement, he helped ex-kicker Billy Cundiff with his charitable work. What does Cundiff's charity aim to do?

    a. Cure ovarian cancer
    b. Help serve hot meals in various Texas locations
    c. Promote social justice
    d. Support military communities in the U.S. and around the world

18. Chadwick "Chad" Stanley played college football at Stephen F. Austin State University in Texas, was signed as an undrafted free agent by San Francisco, and came to Houston in the 2002 Expansion Draft. What's the team-record number of yards he punted the pigskin while in Houston?

    a. 14,766
    b. 15,957
    c. 16,899

d. 17,908

19. Owen Daniels was drafted in the 4th round (98th overall) in the 2006 NFL Draft. He majored in meteorology at the University of Wisconsin, was nicknamed "The Weatherman," and appeared on the Madison area news delivering the forecast. As a Texan, the moniker "O.D." stuck among Houston fans and media. What's his record for receptions by a Texans tight end in a single season (2008)?

    a. 55
    b. 62
    c. 70
    d. 85

20. In Week 15 of the 2018 season, Fairbairn kicked five field goals and two extra points in a 29-22 win over the New York Jets, earning him AFC Special Teams Player of the Week. He set the Houston record that year for most field goals made. Out of 42 attempts, how many did he connect on?

    a. 35
    b. 37
    c. 39
    d. 41

QUIZ ANSWERS

1. C – 2016

2. B – 416

3. D – Tennessee

4. C – 21

5. D – Jon Weeks

6. C – Sage Rosenfels

7. D – Ben Tate

8. A – True

9. B – André Davis

10. A – Kris Brown

11. C – 410

12. B – 23/15

13. B – 5'6" (167.6 cm)

14. A – André Davis

15. B – 108

16. D – Tennessee

17. A – Cure ovarian cancer

18. D – 17,908

19. C – 70

20. B – 37

DID YOU KNOW?

1. On December 7, 2014, Alfred Blue scored his first career rushing touchdown, against the Jaguars. At that moment, Blue became the first player in franchise history with a rushing, receiving, and return touchdown in the same season.

2. As a college senior, Houston record-setter Jon Weeks was voted as Baylor's special teams captain and was widely considered one of the best long snappers in college football. He also chipped in with six tackles and a forced fumble during his collegiate career.

3. Weeks commented on what it meant to surpass Andre Johnson for the record of most consecutive games played by a Texan: "It's a tremendous feeling. Any time you can do anything in this organization that surpasses Andre is surreal. Andre is going to be considered the greatest Texan ever to put on the uniform. I'm just very fortunate to still be out there doing what I love to do and playing with these guys and enjoying every Sunday, and not taking a moment for granted."

4. Chester Morise Pitts II was the focus of the NFL SuperAd commercial shown during Super Bowl XLII detailing the story of how his career got started. In addition, he set the all-time Houston franchise record by participating in 3,884 straight snaps.

5. Speaking of record attendance at home, Houston's December 7, 2008, home game against the Tennessee Titans saw a then-record crowd of 70,831. The home finale on December 28, 2008, against the Chicago Bears drew a franchise-record mass of 70,838 fans. That record was broken on November 23, 2009, when a new record crowd of 71,153 was in attendance during Houston's second *Monday Night Football* appearance against the former NFL team from Houston, the Tennessee Titans.

6. Houston kicker Kris Brown was a four-year starter and won two national championships at the University of Nebraska. Brown broke multiple school records while playing for the Cornhuskers, including most career points (388), most field goals made (217), most consecutive field goals made (17), most PATs made (217), most consecutive PATs made (114), and most points scored by a kicker during a season (116), among others.

7. Brian Cushing was Houston's tackling master, setting records for total tackles (658) and assists on tackles (238). Cushing and Archie Griffin of the Ohio State University Buckeyes are the only two players in college football history to have competed in the Rose Bowl as starters in all four seasons of their college careers.

8. J.J. Moses handled a record number of kick returns for the Texans (117) and also played for the Scottish Claymores of NFL Europe, where he was the number-one punt returner for the 2002 season. J.J. is currently director of player engagement with Houston.

9. In his rookie season with Houston, Jerome Mathis was selected to the Pro Bowl as the AFC's starting kick returner. He was one of three rookies (linebacker Shawne Merriman of the Chargers and linebacker Lofa Tatupu of the Seahawks being the others) selected to participate in the game.

CHAPTER 12:

BRING ON THE RIVALS

QUIZ TIME!

1. In recent history, who has been Deshaun Watson's main in-state competition to be the best young quarterback in the Lone Star State?

   a. Troy Aikman
   b. Dak Preston
   c. Tony Romo
   d. Tyrod Taylor

2. The AFC divisional contest between Houston and Kansas City in January 2020 showcased high-powered offenses under the guidance of youthful star quarterbacks (Watson and Patrick Mahomes), even though Kansas City has a 7-5 edge in the series. How many points did the Chiefs spot the Texans in that game before storming back to win, 51-31?

   a. 21
   b. 24

c. 28

d. 31

3. The Indianapolis Colts can be considered one of the toughest AFC Division rivals for Houston, especially since they play at least twice a year. What was the advantage that Indy held in the series between the two teams as of 2020?

  a. 19-18
  b. 22-15
  c. 25-12
  d. 28-9

4. What was the name of the Houston Oilers' owner who openly threatened to move the franchise to Tennessee since the late 1980s and finally made good on his word in 1996?

  a. Bud Adams
  b. Bob Brodhead
  c. Pop Ivy
  d. Bum Phillips

5. At the end of the '80s, the Houston Oilers' owner expressed his displeasure with the team's crumbling accommodations at the old Astrodome. When he claimed his dream wasn't being realized, which city did he threaten to move his team to?

  a. Anchorage
  b. Jacksonville

c. Las Vegas

d. Tampa Bay-St. Petersburg

6. Playing their first season in 1995 together with the Carolina Panthers, the rival Jacksonville Jaguars don't predate the Texans by much—just seven seasons. The only other team that shares this type of relative "newness" in the NFL is the Baltimore Ravens, who began official league play in 1999.

a. True

b. False

7. Many long-term Houstonians still recall having to spend their hard-earned tax dollars on Astrodome renovations and then having the Oilers' owner pull the plug anyway and move to Tennessee less than 10 years after the Dome was renovated. What word do they often use to describe their feelings?

a. Angst

b. Apathy

c. Bemusement

d. Betrayal

8. The Texans had never managed to beat the Colts in Indianapolis until the 2015 season. Another reason for some of the bitterness between the two teams was the "Houston native" quarterback that led the Colts for years. Who was he?

a. Bert Jones

b. Andrew Luck

c. Peyton Manning

d. Philip Rivers

9. The Texans have an intrastate rivalry with the Dallas Cowboys. They face each other every year in a special game (a tradition that began between the cities before the Oilers relocating) that takes place either in the preseason or the regular season for bragging rights in the great state of Texas. What's the game called?

a. The Big D-Space City Showdown

b. The Governor's Cup

c. The Lone Star Challenge

d. The War for Texas

10. 1The aforementioned battle for football supremacy in the state was first temporarily moved to Arlington and finally canceled in Week 4 of 2017 due to the extensive damage done by a massive hurricane. Which hurricane caused the cancellation that year?

a. Agnes

b. Harvey

c. Katrina

d. Maria

11. Houston head coach Gary Kubiak had been a ball boy as a kid for the Oilers' beloved Bum Phillips. Which rival team fired Bum's son Wade, allowing Kubiak to sign him to take over as the Texans' defensive coordinator in 2010?

a. Dallas

b. Indianapolis

c. Jacksonville

d. Tennessee

12. Despite tough injuries to receiver Andre Johnson and quarterback Matt Schaub, the Texans played at home in the first-ever playoff game in franchise history on January 7, 2012, in front of 71,725 delirious fans. Which opponent became an "automatic" rival that day as Houston won 31-10?

a. Buffalo Bills

b. Cincinnati Bengals

c. New England Patriots

d. Pittsburgh Steelers

13. In 2015, Houston head man Bill O'Brien and Jacksonville coach Doug Marrone became rivals in the pros, although they were buddies working together under George O'Leary in 1999. Which university had hired both coaches at that earlier time?

a. Auburn

b. Georgia Tech

c. Grambling

d. Louisiana State University

14. Some Houston fans are old enough to remember certain players who were originally drafted by the Houston Oilers but went on to great success with the Titans as a result of the oilmen's move to the Volunteer State. Which of the following is a prime example?

a. David Garrard

b. Rashean Mathis

c. Steve McNair

d. Fred Taylor

15. *Indianapolis's Peyton Manning made Houston's defense his personal playground: he was 16-2 as a starter against the Texans, throwing for 5,122 yards, 42 touchdowns, and only eight interceptions. Also, he completed 70.4% of his passes and had a 110.6 quarterback rating—basically out of this world.*

a. True

b. False

16. According to one pundit, "the *Texans must beat the Baltimore Ravens to get over that AFC hump, and it is their current NFL demon.*" Which of the following players was NOT cast off by Houston, only to be picked up by Baltimore?

a. Eddie George

b. Jacoby Jones

c. Vonta Leach

d. Bernard Pollard

17. Maybe Dallas fans don't feel quite the same animosity toward Texans fans as vice versa. Witness the following: "As a Cowboy fan, I don't get it. I have no feelings toward the Texans until we actually play them. I can't say the same for Texans fans because they get gleeful, damn near _____, when ANY team beats the Cowboys or Tony Romo throws a pick to end a game." What's missing?

a. Gay

b. Giddy

c. Glad

d. Dizzy

18. The Texans began their 2010 season with a home game against the Indianapolis Colts, a division rival that they had only beaten once ever. Houston rolled, 34-24, carried on the huge shoulders of Arian Foster, rambled for 231 yards. Who was the only player who ever gained more in a season opener?

a. Earl Campbell

b. Edgerrin James

c. Walter Payton

d. O.J. Simpson

19. Which former Texans quarterback engineered a Week 16 win over Houston in 2011, as the Colts went 2-14 while the Texans finally took the division? That loss cost the Texans a possible shot at a bye.

a. Jacob Eason

b. Jalen Morton

c. Dan Orlovsky

d. T.J. Yates

20. There's one surefire way to fuel a rivalry: a good old-fashioned fight. In 2010, which Titans' player poked and punched Andre Johnson before the latter ripped off the Tennessee player's helmet, threw him to the ground, and pummeled him?

a. Jason Babin
b. Jed Collins
c. Cortland Finnegan
d. Derrick Morgan

QUIZ ANSWERS

1. B – Dak Preston
2. A – 21
3. D – 28-9
4. A – Bud Adams
5. B – Jacksonville
6. B – False (The Baltimore Ravens actually began to play as a team in 1996.)
7. D – Betrayal
8. B – Andrew Luck
9. B – The Governor's Cup
10. B – Harvey
11. A – Dallas
12. B – Cincinnati Bengals
13. B – Georgia Tech
14. C – Steve McNair
15. A – True
16. A – Eddie George
17. B – Giddy
18. D – O.J. Simpson
19. C – Dan Orlovsky
20. C – Cortland Finnegan

DID YOU KNOW?

1. In the AFC South, the Texans share their division with the Indianapolis Colts, Tennessee Titans, and Jacksonville Jaguars. They have always appeared to be in a fight to win the division right down to the final week of the year.

2. Houston has made the playoffs on six different occasions since 2002, having to play on Wild Card weekend in 2011, 2012, 2015, 2016, 2018, and 2019. They've been able to advance to the Divisional Weekend four of those times.

3. In Houston's inaugural 2002 season, the Texans became only the second team in NFL history to win their first game in the league by defeating their in-state rivals, the Dallas Cowboys, by a score of 19-10. There's nothing quite like beating your cross-state foes; especially, a team that's still sometimes called "America's Team"—where on earth did that come from?

4. The most manageable deficit to overcome between all the teams listed, the Tennessee Titans were ranked as the Texans' top rival, according to an SB Nation fan poll conducted in 2018. The Titans received 63% of the vote, demonstrating that the two middling franchises in the AFC South have been fighting each other tooth and nail for more territory in trying to win the division.

5. What really defines a rival, according to Sean Pendergast of the *Houston Press*? "For the record, in my opinion, in

order to truly be 'rivals', the feeling (read: hatred) between the two teams has to be mutual. In other words, the other team you identify as 'rival' must feel virtually the same way about your team. The sports hate can be based in anything—geography, frequent postseason meetings, stealing a franchise from your city (HELLO, NASHVILLE)—so long as it exists and goes two ways," Sean claims.

6. Could Denver also be seen as a worthy rival of the Texans? "The Texans stole their quarterback. The Broncos gave safe haven to the Texans' entire ousted coaching staff and won a goddamn Super Bowl with them. The Broncos could be the answer to this question if we get a postseason meeting or two over the next few years," Pendergast reasons.

7. The Houston Oilers were a consistent playoff team from 1987 to 1993, a period that included both of the Oilers' only division titles (1991 and 1993), as well as the dubious distinction of being on the losing end of the largest comeback in NFL history, a record that still exists to this day. In a contest also called "The Comeback" or "The Choke," Houston built a 32-point lead only to lose in overtime to Buffalo, 41-38, in 1993.

8. It's safe to say that the Texans have established a kind of dominance against several rivals. Houston is 23-13 all-time against the Jags, which is good enough for a .639 winning percentage. Houston has a better all-time winning

percentage than that against six other select teams: the Dolphins (.889), Buccaneers (.800), Lions (.750), Browns (.700), Raiders (.666 including playoffs), and Bengals (.666 including playoffs).

9. On the other hand, there are a few franchises that the Texans apparently would prefer not to tangle with. For starters, against the Colts the Texans boast a .243 total losing percentage. To give this some context, Houston has a worse all-time losing percentage against just five other teams: the Vikings (.000), Eagles (.000), Patriots (.166 including playoffs), Ravens (.181 including playoffs), and Giants (.200).

10. But now that Peyton Manning has gracefully left Indianapolis, maybe Houston has a fighting chance. From 1998 to 2011, Peyton was the signal-caller for the Colts in 20 games against Houston. He and his team went 17-3 against the Texans during those 20 contests. In one of those three Houston wins, Manning didn't even play because of neck injuries and surgeries (Kerry Collins did his best instead.).

CONCLUSION

If we've done our job correctly, you've reached this point chock-full of new facts about your favorite NFL team, the Houston Texans. Whether it's the notable players who hold franchise records or some of the behind-the-scenes information about how some of your favorite stars arrived in "Clutch City," we hope you enjoyed this trip down memory lane and through the brief but rich history of the Texans.

We've done our best to cover it all for you from the Texans' entrance into the NFL in 2002, to their first AFC South division championship and playoff win, in addition to some of the darker days in the franchise's history.

In the Super Bowl era, Houston has had its fair share of highlights, but there have been some lean years in "Space City" as well. Throughout the Texans' storied history, some of the best players ever to play the pro game have done so with the franchise. They might not have quite as many Lombardi Trophies yet as you'd like, but the Texans are an integral part of the fabric of the league we know and love.

This book is designed for you, the fans, to embrace your favorite team and feel closer to them. Maybe you weren't totally familiar with franchise history. Perhaps you were unaware of the success Houston has had in such a brief time in the NFL. Maybe you didn't realize just how shrewdly the Texans used and traded their draft picks to try to pick up new talent.

Or perhaps we couldn't stump you at all: You're the ultimate super-fan! No matter how well you did on the quizzes, we hope we captured the spirit of the red, white, and blue Texans, and inspired even more pride in your team.

The Houston Texans are one of the up-and-coming teams in the league. As always, they'll continue to give it their all. It's "Football Time in Houston," as the fight song goes. We're still working on a great new catch phrase for next year. Stay tuned!

www.ingramcontent.com/pod-product-compliance
Lightning Source LLC
Chambersburg PA
CBHW060239030426
42335CB00014B/1537